ROBERT S. MURPHY

NEW
FUN
FLAVOR

Optimal Levels!

Deeper
Understanding
Books

BOOK 1

All graphics and layouts by Robert S. Murphy
Optimal Levels! is based on CREAME pedagogy
(Consciousness Raising, Emotions Analysis, Manipulation, and Expression)

CREAME and *Optimal Levels!* designed by Robert S. Murphy

Copyright © 2014 by Robert S. Murphy
Deeper Understanding Books
1-6-12 Ongagawa, Onga-cho
Onga-gun. Fukuoka, Japan 811-4307

www.murphyschool.com

All rights reserved. No part of the material protected by this copy right notice may be reproduced or utilized in any form by any means, electronic or mechanical, including photocopying, recording, or by any information storage and retrieval system, without written permission from the copyright holder.

Printed in the United States of America

About this series

Welcome to the NEW **OPTIMAL LEVELS!** series. This series is probably unlike any series of textbooks that you have encountered in the past. These textbooks have been designed to maximize student thinking and foster the construction of cognitive skills through the usage of the English language.

"Deeper Understanding" is really about the ability to solve puzzles and problems in the real world. Rather than *presenting* to students what must be learned, this series proposes motivating themes and scaffolded tasks that are designed to build skills systematically and dynamically, from the bottom-up. By doing the theme-based student-centered tasks, students learn and understand language usage by creating the *skills* necessary to negotiate meaning and build upon what they already know.

Enjoy exploring the creation of these dynamic skills that will lead to the *deeper understanding* of English and beyond!

Robert S. Murphy, series author
Deeper Understanding Books

NEW OPTIMAL LEVELS! FUN FLAVOR BOOK 1

Modules	Themes	Grammar Focus
Module 1	Future Travels	Future
Module 2	Movies I have seen	Past
Module 3	Shopping	Present

SELF-ASSESSMENT SHEET (PRE)

NAME: DATE:

	LEVEL (1-5 stars)	COMMENT:
Reading	☆ ☆ ☆ ☆ ☆	_____
Writing	☆ ☆ ☆ ☆ ☆	_____
Listening	☆ ☆ ☆ ☆ ☆	_____
Speaking	☆ ☆ ☆ ☆ ☆	_____
Grammar	☆ ☆ ☆ ☆ ☆	_____
Vocabulary	☆ ☆ ☆ ☆ ☆	_____
Spelling	☆ ☆ ☆ ☆ ☆	_____
Presentations	☆ ☆ ☆ ☆ ☆	_____
Overall Fluency	☆ ☆ ☆ ☆ ☆	_____

About me!

Name:

Cycle 1. Production: Word Map

In groups choose "A" or "B" for your study topic. Create a word map. Connect words/phrases you would need to discuss this topic. ヒント：特にディスカションで使いそうな単語・熟語をどんどん繋げよう！

⊕ positive
⊖ negative

Cycle 2. Exchange: Partner's advice

Exchange books with a partner. Think of better words and give advice.
ヒント：特にディスカションに必要そうな単語を考えてレベルアップさせよう！

Teacher's Approval

許可マーク

Cycle 3a. Production: Word categories

Group work. Use your word maps to create four word lists on this topic.
ヒント：グループワークで助け合い、最強のワードリストを作ろう！

A Cultural Connections
文化的なつながり

B Feelings & Emotions
感情のつながり

Future Travels!
Root Word

C Connections to Society
社会的なつながり

D Phrases & Idioms
フレーズ・熟語

Partner's Approval
許可マーク

Cycle 3b. Production: Context

Copy the words from 3A. Create good sentences as "Grammar Templates".
ヒント：文法テンプレートの作成。3aの単語から「基本」となる文章を作ろう！

Cultural Connections 文化的なつながり

Word/phrase	Sentence with context!

Feelings & Emotions 感情のつながり

Word/phrase	Sentence with context!

Partner's Approval
許可マーク

Cycle 3b. Production: Context

Copy the words from 3A. Create good sentences as "Grammar Templates".
ヒント：文法テンプレートの作成。3aの単語から「基本」となる文章を作ろう！

Connections to Society 社会的なつながり

Word/phrase	Sentence with context!

Phrases & Idioms フレーズ・熟語

Word/phrase	Sentence with context!

Partner's Approval
許可マーク

Cycle 4a. Exchange: Lexical ideas from the teacher

 View teachers lists. Copy them here! Think and compare with your list.
先生のリストを写して、自分のリストとの違いを探ろう！

A. Cultural Connections
文化的なつながり

on my list YES/NO	on my list YES/NO
on my list YES/NO	on my list YES/NO
on my list YES/NO	on my list YES/NO
on my list YES/NO	on my list YES/NO

B. Feelings
感情のつながり

on my list YES/NO	on my list YES/NO
on my list YES/NO	on my list YES/NO
on my list YES/NO	on my list YES/NO
on my list YES/NO	on my list YES/NO

Future Travels! — Root Word

C. Connections to society
社会的なつながり

on my list YES/NO	on my list YES/NO
on my list YES/NO	on my list YES/NO
on my list YES/NO	on my list YES/NO
on my list YES/NO	on my list YES/NO

D. Phrases & Idioms
フレーズ・熟語

on my list YES/NO	on my list YES/NO
on my list YES/NO	on my list YES/NO
on my list YES/NO	on my list YES/NO
on my list YES/NO	on my list YES/NO

 Partner's Approval
許可マーク

Cycle 4b. Exchange: Grammar Ideas from the teacher

View teachers "Grammar Template" examples. Copy them here! Think and compare with your list.
先生のリストを写して、自分のリストとの違いを探ろう！

Future Travels!

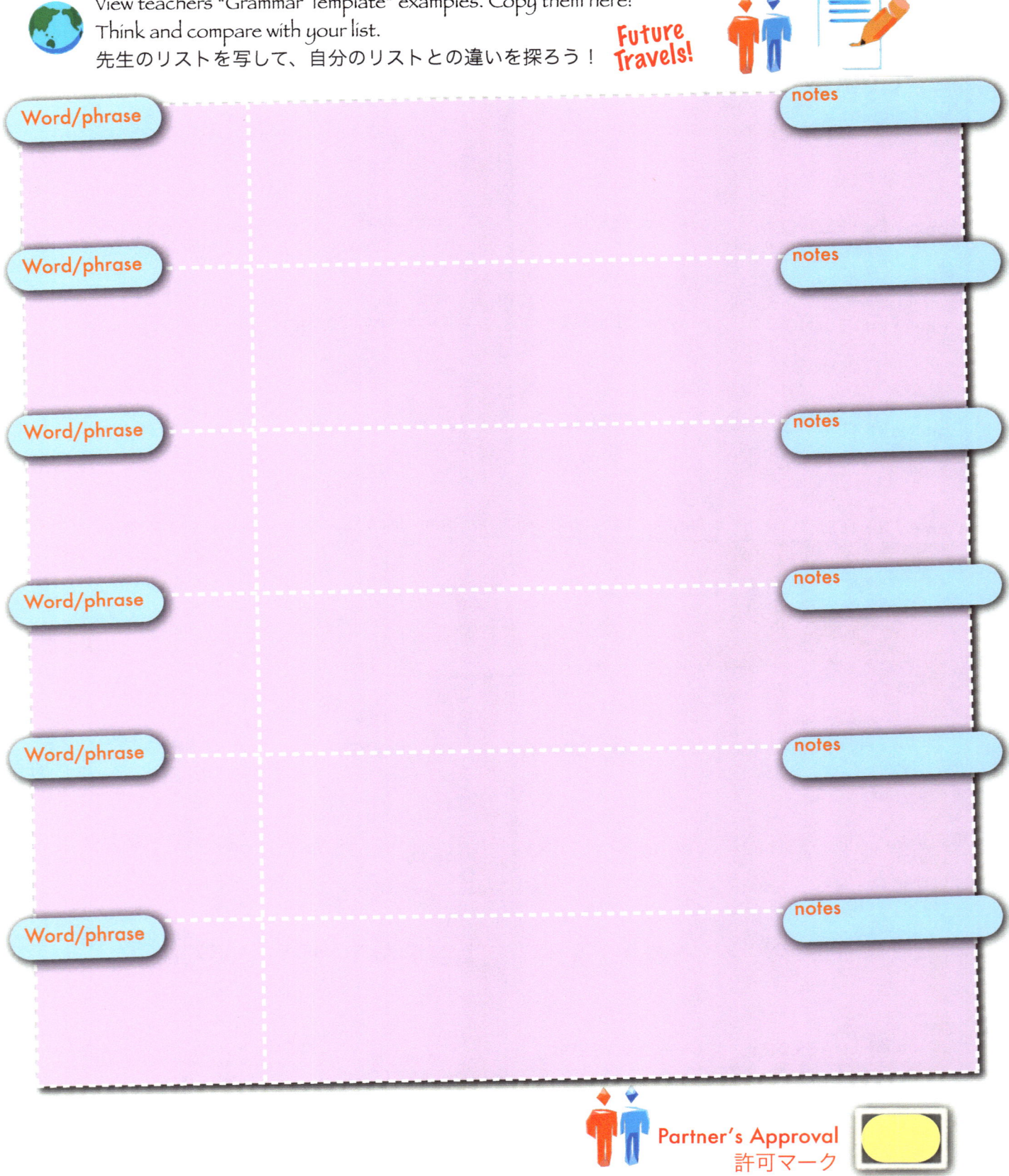

Partner's Approval
許可マーク

Cycle 5a. Production – Group Master List!

Create a Master List with your group! Mix your ideas with your teacher's ideas.
ヒント：２つのリストを比べて、グループで話し合い、最強のリストを作ろう！

Phrases	Culture	Feelings	Society

List three of your best "Grammar Template" sentences for this topic. 文法の例文となるsentences!

A

B

C

Show this group list to the class with your teacher's help (on screen).

Cycle 5b. Class Grammar Templates List

Mix your ideas from the whole class. Write down ten great template sentences for this topic.
ヒント：最強の文法・例文となるテンプレートリストを作ろう！

Design your own "Grammar Boxes" ヒント：自分のためになるGrammar Boxを作ろう

Future Travels!

Grammar box A:

Grammar box B:

Grammar box C:

Teacher's Approval
許可マーク

Cycle 6. Group-owned: Presentation!

In groups decide presentation content. Practice outside of class, too!
ヒント：プレゼンの内容をよく話し合って、楽しく教室外で何度も練習をしよう！

Slide 1

Theme:

Word/phrase list

Slide 2

Theme:

Word/phrase list

Cycle 6. Group-owned: Presentation!

In groups decide presentation content. Practice outside of class, too!
ヒント：プレゼンの内容をよく話し合って、楽しく教室外で何度も練習をしよう！

Future Travels!

Slide 3

Theme:

Word/phrase list

Slide 4

Theme:

Word/phrase list

Cycle 6. Group-owned: Presentation!

In groups decide presentation content. Practice outside of class, too!
ヒント：プレゼンの内容をよく話し合って、楽しく教室外で何度も練習をしよう！

Slide 5

Theme:

Word/phrase list

Slide 6

Theme:

Word/phrase list

Cycle 7. Presentation Feedback

Listen to the group presentations. Assess performance. Score fairly! Add your learning points from them.
ヒント：他のグループのプレゼンの良い/悪い所を細かくチェック！学べる所もあるはずー＞Learning Point

	Vocabulary 単語レベル	Fluency 流暢レベル	Grammar 文法レベル	Captivating 魅了的内容	Logical Flow 論理的流れ
Group A	1..2..3..4..5	1..2..3..4..5	1..2..3..4..5	1..2..3..4..5	1..2..3..4..5
Learning point ▶					
Group B	1..2..3..4..5	1..2..3..4..5	1..2..3..4..5	1..2..3..4..5	1..2..3..4..5
Learning point ▶					
Group C	1..2..3..4..5	1..2..3..4..5	1..2..3..4..5	1..2..3..4..5	1..2..3..4..5
Learning point ▶					
Group D	1..2..3..4..5	1..2..3..4..5	1..2..3..4..5	1..2..3..4..5	1..2..3..4..5
Learning point ▶					
Group E	1..2..3..4..5	1..2..3..4..5	1..2..3..4..5	1..2..3..4..5	1..2..3..4..5
Learning point ▶					
Group F	1..2..3..4..5	1..2..3..4..5	1..2..3..4..5	1..2..3..4..5	1..2..3..4..5
Learning point ▶					

Future Travels!

Cycle 7b. Presentation: Feedback notes

Use this area to write down notes about the presentations!

Today's best performance! ➡ Group

Cycle 8. Group work: Design a test! (Page 1)

In your groups, design a test! Consider your Master Lists, your Grammar Boxes, and the Learning Points!

Name_____ Student Number_____ Date_____ Class_____

MODULE 1. TEST TITLE: _____

Future Travels!

Section 1:

Section 2:

Cycle 8. Group work: Design a test! (Page 2)

ヒント：今までの学習内容を中心に、自分を高めるためのテストをデザイン！

Name_____ Student Number_____ Date_____ Class_____

MODULE 1. TEST TITLE: _____

Future Travels!

Section 3.

Section 4.

Show this group test to the class with your teacher's help (on screen). The best test becomes the official test!

ヒント：選ばれたテストが実際にクラステストとして使われる！自分のテストが選ばれたら、絶対にトク！

Cycle 9. Choice: Best Test Design Award!

Use these charts to choose the best test for the class! 審査と受賞！

	Word choice	Difficulty	Design
Group A	1..2..3..4..5	1..2..3..4..5	1..2..3..4..5
Group B	1..2..3..4..5	1..2..3..4..5	1..2..3..4..5
Group C	1..2..3..4..5	1..2..3..4..5	1..2..3..4..5
Group D	1..2..3..4..5	1..2..3..4..5	1..2..3..4..5
Group E	1..2..3..4..5	1..2..3..4..5	1..2..3..4..5
Group F	1..2..3..4..5	1..2..3..4..5	1..2..3..4..5

	Comments about the test:
Group A	
Group B	
Group C	
Group D	
Group E	
Group F	

Cycle 10. Testing, Reflection, and New Plans!

PART A: Take the Master Test that your class has chosen as the best test for you.
ヒント：みんなで選んだテストを受けよう。

 My test score!

PART B: Think about your presentations and the test. Write down advice for raising your skills further.
ヒント：プレゼンとテストの結果をみて、さらなる実力アップのためにできることを考えよう！

PART C: Discuss your ideas in class with your teacher. Write down new ideas. Make a learning plan.
ヒント：新たなラーニングプランを作成！次のレベルへステップアップ！

New Plan for Study	What do I need to do?

 Teacher's Approval
許可マーク

OPTIONAL

THINK AGAIN

*Think about the module you just finished. Interview a partner.
Write down your combined answers.*
ヒント：パートナーと自分の考えをここでまとめよう！

1. What did you enjoy about this unit?

2. How can you connect what you learned to the real world?

3. What have you become interested in because of this unit?

4. List any new ideas for improving your skills:

low   high
Self-assessment: 1 2 3 4 5

Cycle 1. Production: Word Map

In groups choose "A" or "B" for your study topic. Create a word map. Connect words/phrases you would need to discuss this topic. ヒント：特にディスカッションで使いそうな単語・熟語をどんどん繋げよう！

⊕ positive
⊖ negative

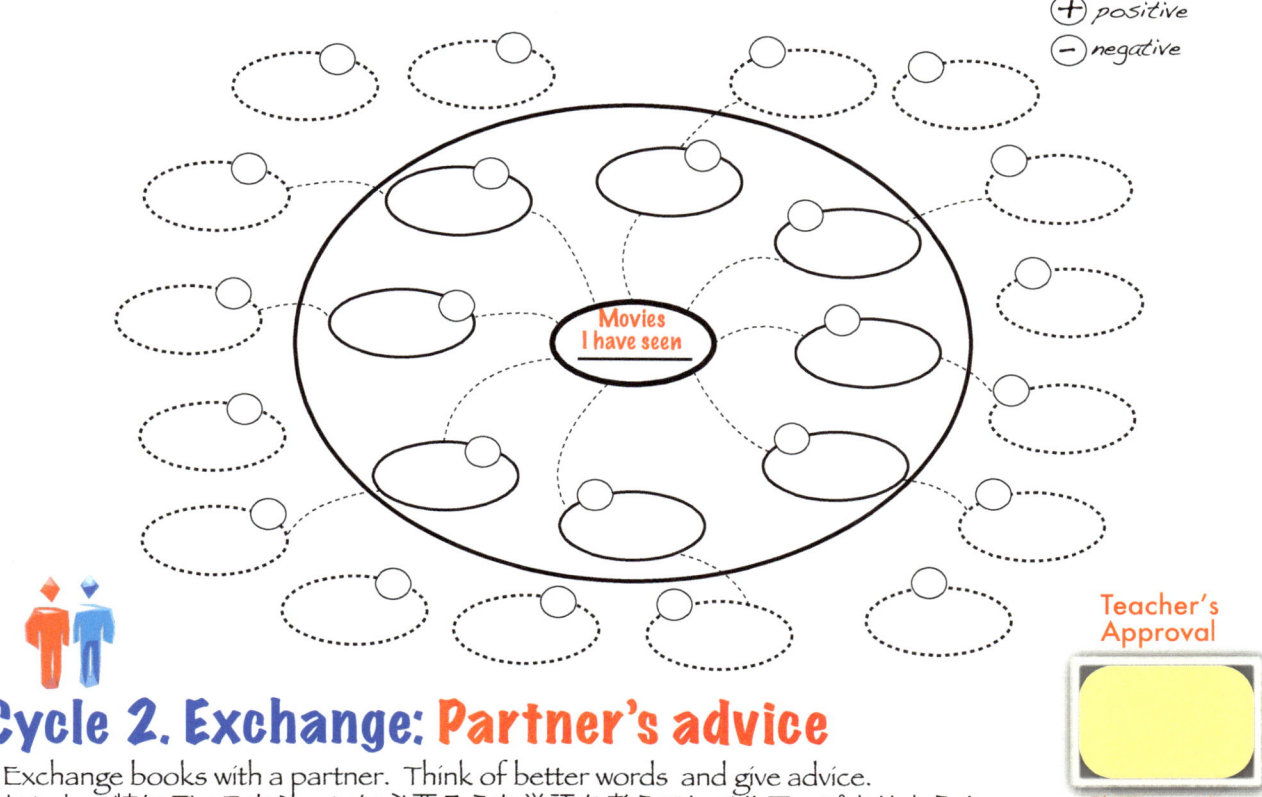

Cycle 2. Exchange: Partner's advice

Exchange books with a partner. Think of better words and give advice.
ヒント：特にディスカッションに必要そうな単語を考えてレベルアップさせよう！

Teacher's Approval

許可マーク

Cycle 3a. Production: Word categories

Group work. Use your word maps to create four word lists on this topic.
ヒント：グループワークで助け合い、最強のワードリストを作ろう！

A Cultural Connections
文化的なつながり

B Feelings & Emotions
感情のつながり

Movies I have seen!
Root Word

C Connections to Society
社会的なつながり

D Phrases & Idioms
フレーズ・熟語

Partner's Approval
許可マーク

Cycle 3b. Production: Context

Copy the words from 3A. Create good sentences as "Grammar Templates".
ヒント：文法テンプレートの作成。3aの単語から、「基本」となる文章を作ろう！

Cultural Connections 文化的なつながり

Word/phrase	Sentence with context!

Feelings & Emotions 感情のつながり

Word/phrase	Sentence with context!

Partner's Approval
許可マーク

Cycle 3b. Production: Context

 Copy the words from 3A. Create good sentences as "Grammar Templates".
ヒント：文法テンプレートの作成。とにかく、基本となる文章を作成！

Connections to Society 社会的なつながり

Word/phrase	Sentence with context!

Phrases & Idioms フレーズ・熟語

Word/phrase	Sentence with context!

Partner's Approval
許可マーク

Cycle 4a. Exchange: Lexical ideas from the teacher

View teachers lists. Copy them here! Think and compare with your list.
先生のリストを写して、自分のリストとの違いを探ろう！

A. Cultural Connections 文化的なつながり

- on my list YES/NO
- on my list YES/NO
- on my list YES/NO
- on my list YES/NO
- on my list YES/NO
- on my list YES/NO
- on my list YES/NO
- on my list YES/NO

B. Feelings 感情のつながり

- on my list YES/NO
- on my list YES/NO
- on my list YES/NO
- on my list YES/NO
- on my list YES/NO
- on my list YES/NO
- on my list YES/NO
- on my list YES/NO

Movies I have seen! Root Word

C. Connections to society 社会的なつながり

- on my list YES/NO
- on my list YES/NO
- on my list YES/NO
- on my list YES/NO
- on my list YES/NO
- on my list YES/NO
- on my list YES/NO
- on my list YES/NO

D. Phrases & Idioms フレーズ・熟語

- on my list YES/NO
- on my list YES/NO
- on my list YES/NO
- on my list YES/NO
- on my list YES/NO
- on my list YES/NO
- on my list YES/NO
- on my list YES/NO

Partner's Approval 許可マーク

Cycle 4b. Exchange: Grammar Ideas from the teacher

View teachers "Grammar Template" examples. Copy them here! Think and compare with your list.
先生のリストを写して、自分のリストとの違いを探ろう！

Movies I have seen!

Word/phrase	notes

Partner's Approval
許可マーク

Cycle 5a. Production – Group Master List!

Create a Master List with your group! Mix your ideas with your teacher's ideas.
ヒント：２つのリストを比べて、グループで話し合い、最強のリストを作ろう！

Phrases	Culture	Feelings	Society

List three of your best "Grammar Template" sentences for this topic. 文法の例文となるsentences!

A

B

C

Show this group list to the class with your teacher's help (on screen).

 Partner's Approval 許可マーク

Cycle 5b. Class Grammar Templates List

Mix your ideas from the whole class. Write down ten great template sentences for this topic.
ヒント：最強の文法・例文となるテンプレートリストを作ろう！

Design your own "Grammar Boxes" ヒント：自分のためになるGrammar Boxを作ろう

Movies I have seen!

Grammar box A:

Grammar box B:

Grammar box C:

Teacher's Approval
許可マーク

Cycle 6. Group-owned: Presentation!

In groups decide presentation content. Practice outside of class, too!
ヒント：プレゼンの内容をよく話し合って、楽しく教室外で何度も練習をしよう！

English in My Past!

Slide 1

Theme:

Word/phrase list

Slide 2

Theme:

Word/phrase list

Cycle 6. Group-owned: Presentation!

In groups decide presentation content. Practice outside of class, too!
ヒント：プレゼンの内容をよく話し合って、楽しく教室外で何度も練習をしよう！

Movies I have seen!

Slide 3

Theme:

Word/phrase list
_____
_____
_____
_____
_____
_____
_____
_____
_____

Slide 4

Theme:

Word/phrase list
_____
_____
_____
_____
_____
_____
_____
_____
_____
_____

Cycle 6. Group-owned: Presentation!

In groups decide presentation content. Practice outside of class, too!
ヒント：プレゼンの内容をよく話し合って、楽しく教室外で何度も練習をしよう！

Slide 5

Theme:

Word/phrase list
_____
_____
_____
_____
_____
_____
_____
_____

Slide 6

Theme:

Word/phrase list
_____
_____
_____
_____
_____
_____
_____
_____

Cycle 7. Presentation Feedback

Listen to the group presentations. Assess performance. Score fairly! Add your learning points from them.
ヒント：他のグループのプレゼンの良い/悪い所を細かくチェック！学べる所もあるはずー＞Learning Point

	Vocabulary 単語レベル	Fluency 流暢レベル	Grammar 文法レベル	Captivating 魅了的内容	Logical Flow 論理的流れ
Group A / Learning point ▶	1..2..3..4..5	1..2..3..4..5	1..2..3..4..5	1..2..3..4..5	1..2..3..4..5
Group B / Learning point ▶	1..2..3..4..5	1..2..3..4..5	1..2..3..4..5	1..2..3..4..5	1..2..3..4..5
Group C / Learning point ▶	1..2..3..4..5	1..2..3..4..5	1..2..3..4..5	1..2..3..4..5	1..2..3..4..5
Group D / Learning point ▶	1..2..3..4..5	1..2..3..4..5	1..2..3..4..5	1..2..3..4..5	1..2..3..4..5
Group E / Learning point ▶	1..2..3..4..5	1..2..3..4..5	1..2..3..4..5	1..2..3..4..5	1..2..3..4..5
Group F / Learning point ▶	1..2..3..4..5	1..2..3..4..5	1..2..3..4..5	1..2..3..4..5	1..2..3..4..5

Movies I have seen!

Cycle 7b. Presentation: Feedback notes

Use this area to write down notes about the presentations!

Today's best performance! → Group

Cycle 8. Group work: Design a test! (Page 1)

In your groups, design a test! Consider your Master Lists, your Grammar Boxes, and the Learning Points!

Name_____ Student Number_____ Date_____ Class_____

MODULE 1. TEST TITLE: _____

Movies I have seen!

Section 1:

Section 2:

Cycle 8. Group work: Design a test! (Page 2)

ヒント：今までの学習内容を中心に、自分を高めるためのテストをデザイン！

Name_____ Student Number_____ Date_____ Class_____

MODULE 1. TEST TITLE: _____

Movies I have seen!

Section 3.

Section 4.

Show this group test to the class with your teacher's help (on screen). The best test becomes the official test!
ヒント：選ばれたテストが実際にクラステストとして使われる！自分のテストが選ばれたら、絶対にトク！

Cycle 9. Choice: Best Test Design Award!

Use these charts to choose the best test for the class! 審査と受賞！

	Word choice	Difficulty	Design
Group A	1..2..3..4..5	1..2..3..4..5	1..2..3..4..5
Group B	1..2..3..4..5	1..2..3..4..5	1..2..3..4..5
Group C	1..2..3..4..5	1..2..3..4..5	1..2..3..4..5
Group D	1..2..3..4..5	1..2..3..4..5	1..2..3..4..5
Group E	1..2..3..4..5	1..2..3..4..5	1..2..3..4..5
Group F	1..2..3..4..5	1..2..3..4..5	1..2..3..4..5

	Comments about the test:
Group A	
Group B	
Group C	
Group D	
Group E	
Group F	

Cycle 10. Testing, Reflection, and New Plans!

PART A: Take the Master Test that your class has chosen as the best test for you.
ヒント：みんなで選んだを受けよう！

 My test score!

PART B: Think about your presentations and the test. Write down advice for raising your skills further.
ヒント：プレゼンとテストの結果をみて、さらなる実力アップのためにできることを考えよう！

Learning point ▶

Learning point ▶

Learning point ▶

Learning point ▶

Learning point ▶

PART C: Discuss your ideas in class with your teacher. Write down new ideas. Make a learning plan.
ヒント：新たなラーニング プランを作成！次のレベルへステップアップ！

New Plan for Study	What do I need to do?

 Teacher's Approval
許可マーク

OPTIONAL

THINK AGAIN

Think about the module you just finished. Interview a partner.
Write down your combined answers.
ヒント：パートナーと自分の考えをここでまとめよう！

1. What did you enjoy about this unit?

2. How can you connect what you learned to the real world?

3. What have you become interested in because of this unit?

4. List any new ideas for improving your skills:

low　high
Self-assessment: 1 2 3 4 5

Module 3 — Shopping!

Cycle 1. Production: Word Map

In groups choose "A" or "B" for your study topic. Create a word map. Connect words/phrases you would need to discuss this topic. ヒント：特にディスカションで使いそうな単語・熟語をどんどん繋げよう！

⊕ positive
⊖ negative

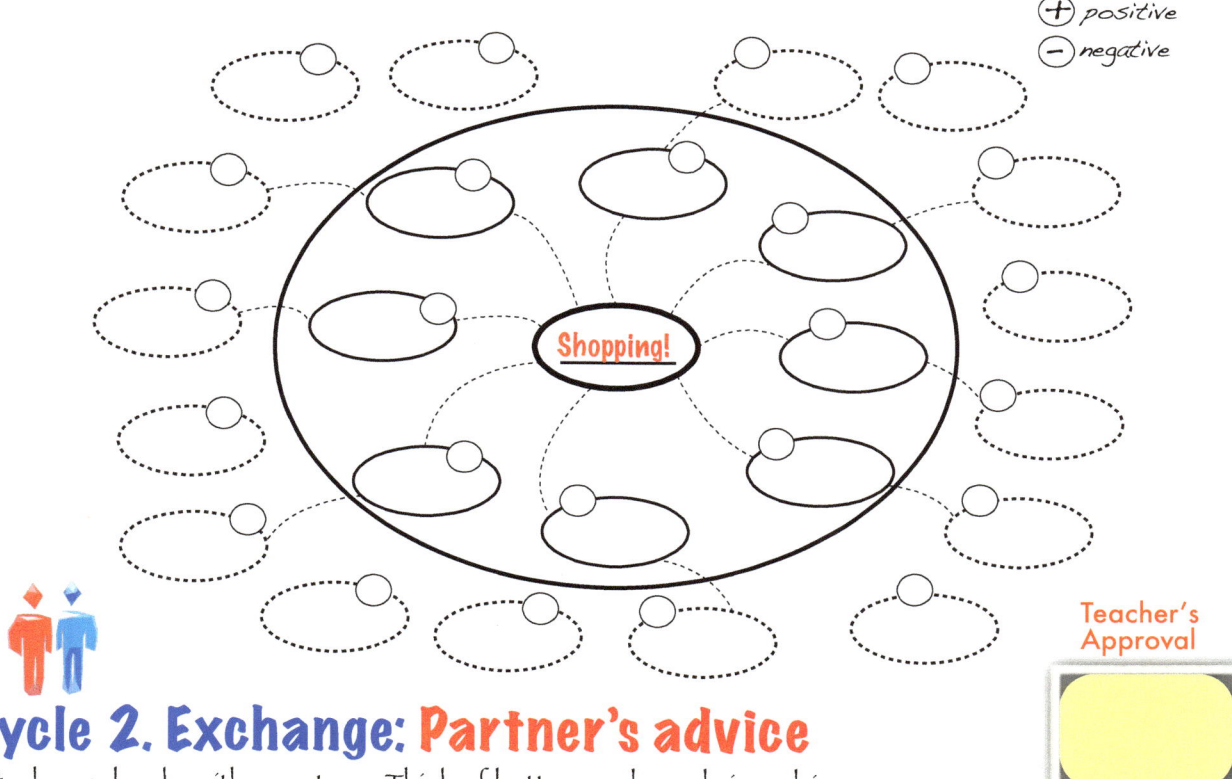

Cycle 2. Exchange: Partner's advice

Exchange books with a partner. Think of better words and give advice.
ヒント：特にディスカションに必要そうな単語を考えてレベルアップさせよう！

Teacher's Approval

許可マーク

Cycle 3a. Production: Word categories

Group work. Use your word maps to create four word lists on this topic.
ヒント：グループワークで助け合い、最強のワードリストを作ろう！

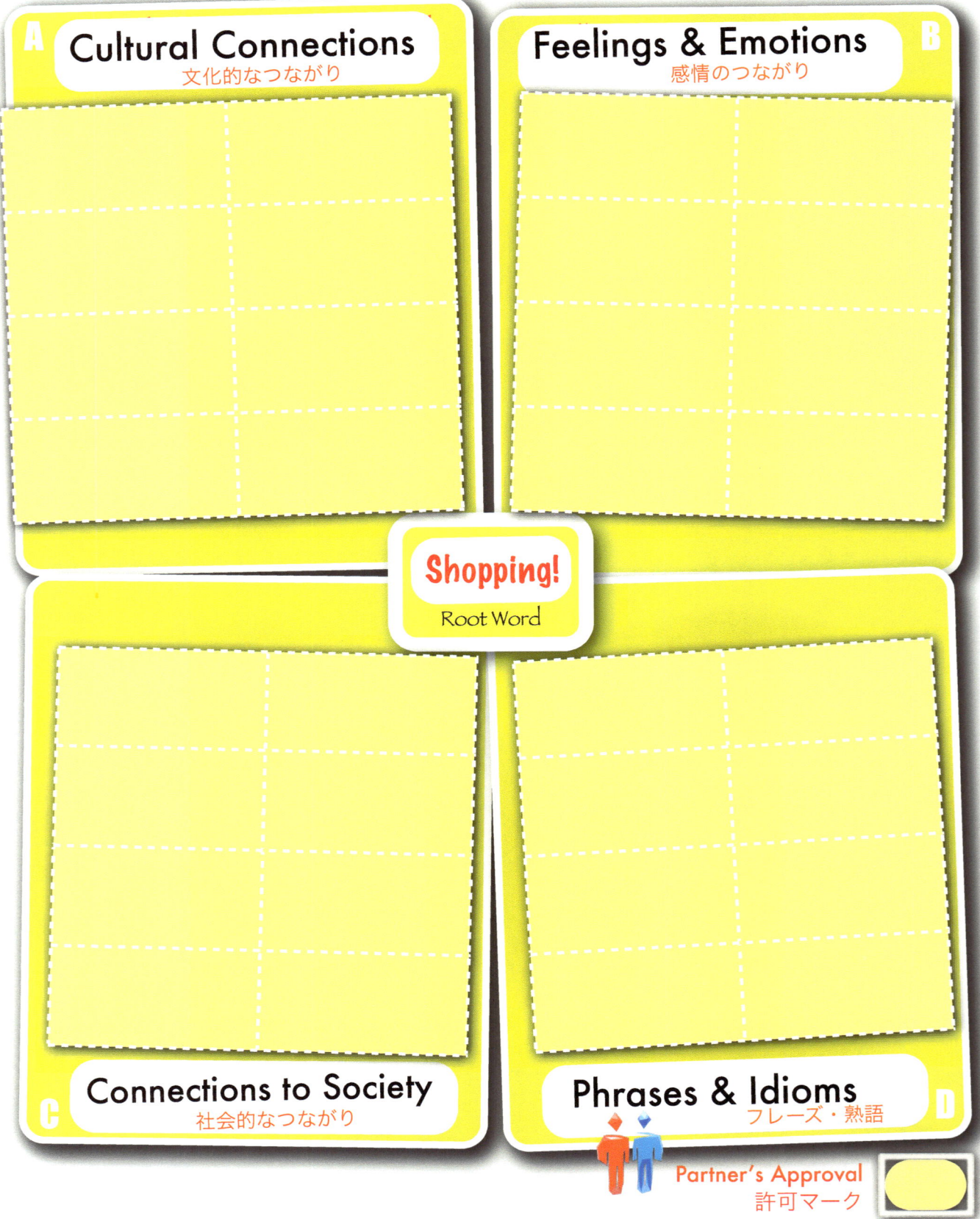

A Cultural Connections
文化的なつながり

B Feelings & Emotions
感情のつながり

Shopping!
Root Word

C Connections to Society
社会的なつながり

D Phrases & Idioms
フレーズ・熟語

Partner's Approval
許可マーク

Cycle 3b. Production: Context

Copy the words from 3A. Create good sentences as "Grammar Templates".
ヒント：文法テンプレートの作成。3aの単語から、「基本」となる文章を作ろう！

Cultural Connections 文化的なつながり

Word/phrase	Sentence with context!

Feelings & Emotions 感情のつながり

Word/phrase	Sentence with context!

Partner's Approval 許可マーク

Cycle 3b. Production: Context

Copy the words from 3A. Create good sentences as "Grammar Templates".
ヒント：文法テンプレートの作成。3aの単語から、「基本」となる文章を作ろう！

Connections to Society 社会的なつながり

Word/phrase	Sentence with context!

Phrases & Idioms フレーズ・熟語

Word/phrase	Sentence with context!

Partner's Approval 許可マーク

Cycle 4a. Exchange: Lexical ideas from the teacher

 View teachers lists. Copy them here! Think and compare with your list.
先生のリストを写して、自分のリストとの違いを探ろう！

A — Cultural Connections
文化的なつながり

- on my list YES/NO
- on my list YES/NO
- on my list YES/NO
- on my list YES/NO
- on my list YES/NO
- on my list YES/NO
- on my list YES/NO
- on my list YES/NO

B — Feelings
感情のつながり

- on my list YES/NO
- on my list YES/NO
- on my list YES/NO
- on my list YES/NO
- on my list YES/NO
- on my list YES/NO
- on my list YES/NO
- on my list YES/NO

Shopping!
Root Word

C — Connections to society
社会的なつながり

- on my list YES/NO
- on my list YES/NO
- on my list YES/NO
- on my list YES/NO
- on my list YES/NO
- on my list YES/NO
- on my list YES/NO
- on my list YES/NO

D — Phrases & Idioms
フレーズ・熟語

- on my list YES/NO
- on my list YES/NO
- on my list YES/NO
- on my list YES/NO
- on my list YES/NO
- on my list YES/NO
- on my list YES/NO
- on my list YES/NO

Partner's Approval
許可マーク

Cycle 4b. Exchange: Grammar Ideas from the teacher

View teachers "Grammar Template" examples. Copy them here! Think and compare with your list.
先生のリストを写して、自分のリストとの違いを探ろう！

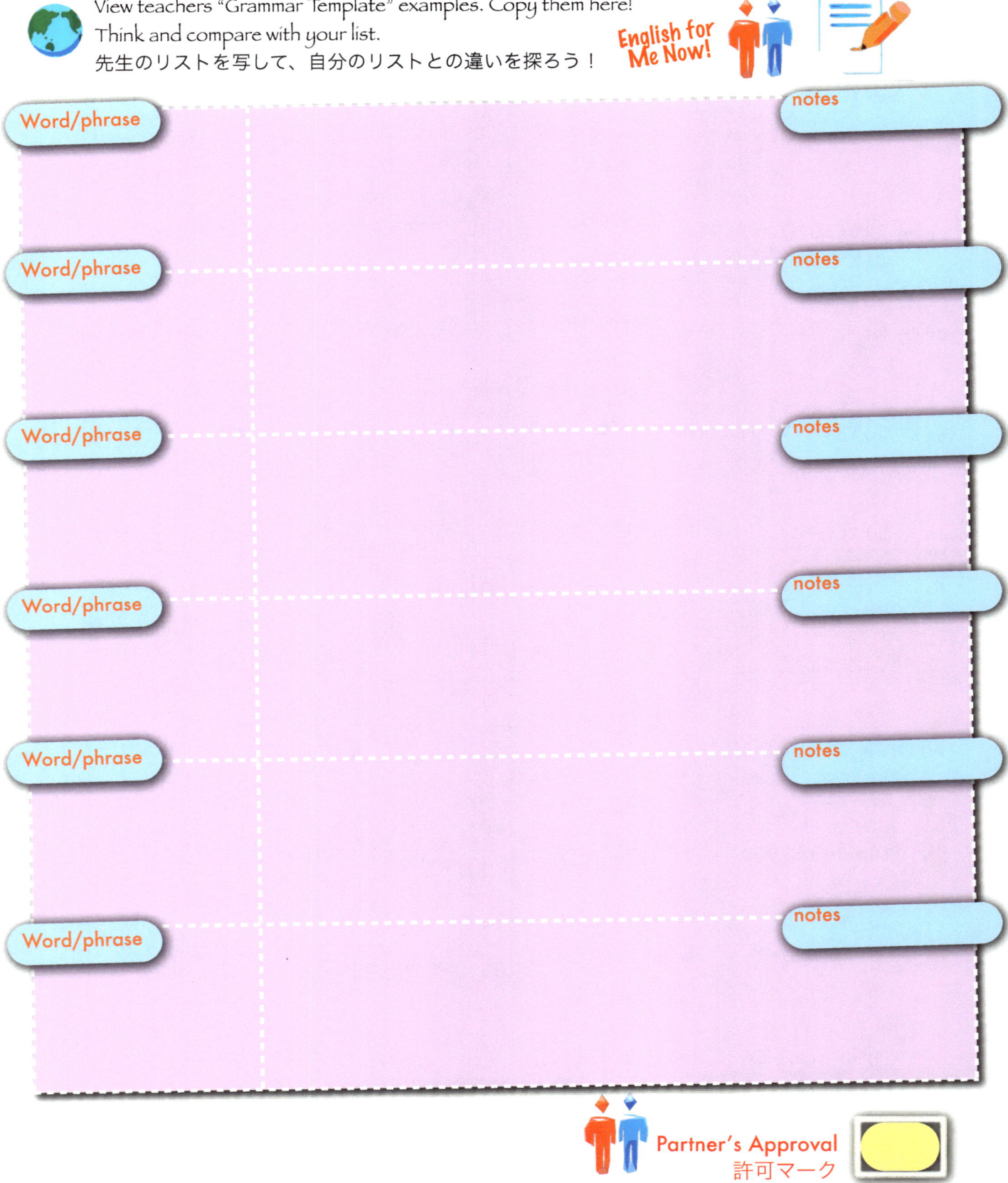

Word/phrase	notes
Word/phrase	notes
Word/phrase	notes
Word/phrase	notes
Word/phrase	notes
Word/phrase	notes

Partner's Approval
許可マーク

Cycle 5a. Production - Group Master List!

Create a Master List with your group! Mix your ideas with your teacher's ideas.
ヒント：２つのリストを比べて、グループで話し合い、最強のリストを作ろう！

Phrases	Culture	Feelings	Society

List three of your best "Grammar Template" sentences for this topic. 文法の例文となるsentences!

A

B

C

Show this group list to the class with your teacher's help (on screen).

Partner's Approval 許可マーク

Cycle 5b. Class Grammar Templates List

Mix your ideas from the whole class. Write down ten great template sentences for this topic.
ヒント：最強の文法・例文となるテンプレートリストを作ろう！

Design your own "Grammar Boxes" ヒント：自分のためになるGrammar Boxを作ろう

Grammar box A:

Grammar box B:

Grammar box C:

Teacher's Approval
許可マーク

Cycle 6. Group-owned: Presentation!

In groups decide presentation content. Practice outside of class, too!
ヒント：プレゼンの内容をよく話し合って、楽しく教室外で何度も練習をしよう！

Slide 1

Theme:

Word/phrase list
_____
_____
_____
_____
_____
_____
_____
_____

Slide 2

Theme:

Word/phrase list
_____
_____
_____
_____
_____
_____
_____
_____

Cycle 6. Group-owned: Presentation!

In groups decide presentation content. Practice outside of class, too!
ヒント：プレゼンの内容をよく話し合って、楽しく教室外で何度も練習をしよう！

Shopping!

Slide 3

Theme:

Word/phrase list
_____
_____
_____
_____
_____
_____
_____
_____

Slide 4

Theme:

Word/phrase list
_____
_____
_____
_____
_____
_____
_____
_____

Cycle 6. Group-owned: Presentation!

In groups decide presentation content. Practice outside of class, too!
ヒント：プレゼンの内容をよく話し合って、楽しく教室外で何度も練習をしよう！

Slide 5

Theme:

Word/phrase list
_____
_____
_____
_____
_____
_____
_____
_____

Slide 6

Theme:

Word/phrase list
_____
_____
_____
_____
_____
_____
_____
_____

Cycle 7. Presentation Feedback

Listen to the group presentations. Assess performance. Score fairly! Add your learning points from them.
ヒント：他のグループのプレゼンの良い/悪い所を細かくチェック！学べる所もあるはずー＞Learning Point

	Vocabulary 単語レベル	Fluency 流暢レベル	Grammar 文法レベル	Captivating 魅了的内容	Logical Flow 論理的流れ
Group A	1..2..3..4..5	1..2..3..4..5	1..2..3..4..5	1..2..3..4..5	1..2..3..4..5
Learning point ▶					
Group B	1..2..3..4..5	1..2..3..4..5	1..2..3..4..5	1..2..3..4..5	1..2..3..4..5
Learning point ▶					
Group C	1..2..3..4..5	1..2..3..4..5	1..2..3..4..5	1..2..3..4..5	1..2..3..4..5
Learning point ▶					
Group D	1..2..3..4..5	1..2..3..4..5	1..2..3..4..5	1..2..3..4..5	1..2..3..4..5
Learning point ▶					
Group E	1..2..3..4..5	1..2..3..4..5	1..2..3..4..5	1..2..3..4..5	1..2..3..4..5
Learning point ▶					
Group F	1..2..3..4..5	1..2..3..4..5	1..2..3..4..5	1..2..3..4..5	1..2..3..4..5
Learning point ▶					

Shopping!

Cycle 7b. Presentation: Feedback notes

Use this area to write down notes about the presentations!

Today's best performance! → Group

Cycle 8. Group work: Design a test! (Page 1)

In your groups, design a test! Consider your Master Lists, your Grammar Boxes, and the Learning Points!

Name_____ Student Number_____ Date_____ Class_____

MODULE 1. TEST TITLE: _____

Shopping!

Section 1:

Section 2:

Cycle 8. Group work: Design a test! (Page 2)

ヒント：今までの学習内容を中心に、自分を高めるためのテストをデザイン！

Name_____ Student Number_____ Date_____ Class_____

MODULE 1. TEST TITLE: _____

Shopping!

Section 3.

Section 4.

Show this group test to the class with your teacher's help (on screen). The best test becomes the official test!

ヒント：選ばれたテストが実際にクラステストとして使われる！自分のテストが選ばれたら、絶対にトク！

Cycle 9. Choice: Best Test Design Award!

Use these charts to choose the best test for the class! 審査と受賞！

	Word choice	Difficulty	Design
Group A	1..2..3..4..5	1..2..3..4..5	1..2..3..4..5
Group B	1..2..3..4..5	1..2..3..4..5	1..2..3..4..5
Group C	1..2..3..4..5	1..2..3..4..5	1..2..3..4..5
Group D	1..2..3..4..5	1..2..3..4..5	1..2..3..4..5
Group E	1..2..3..4..5	1..2..3..4..5	1..2..3..4..5
Group F	1..2..3..4..5	1..2..3..4..5	1..2..3..4..5

	Comments about the test:
Group A	
Group B	
Group C	
Group D	
Group E	
Group F	

Cycle 10. Testing, Reflection, and New Plans!

PART A: Take the Master Test that your class has chosen as the best test for you.
ヒント：まずは選ばれたテストを受けよう！

 Shopping!   My test score!

PART B: Think about your presentations and the test. Write down advice for raising your skills further.
ヒント：プレゼンとテストの結果をみて、さらなる実力アップのためにできることを考えよう！

PART C: Discuss your ideas in class with your teacher. Write down new ideas. Make a learning plan.
ヒント：新たなラーニング プランを作成！次のレベルへステップアップ！

New Plan for Study	What do I need to do?

 Teacher's Approval 許可マーク

OPTIONAL

THINK AGAIN

*Think about the module you just finished. Interview a partner.
Write down your combined answers.*
ヒント：パートナーと自分の考えをここでまとめよう！

1. What did you enjoy about this unit?

2. How can you connect what you learned to the real world?

3. What have you become interested in because of this unit?

4. List any new ideas for improving your skills:

low　　high
Self-assessment: 1 2 3 4 5

Positive Thoughts Journal Day 1

I am happy because:

_____

_____

_____

_____

_____

_____

_____

_____

_____

_____

_____

Positive Thoughts Journal Day 2

I am happy because:
_____

_____

_____

_____

_____

_____

_____

_____

_____

_____

_____

_____

Positive Thoughts Journal Day 3

I am happy because:
_____

_____

_____

_____

_____

_____

_____

_____

_____

_____

_____

_____

Positive Thoughts Journal Day 4

I am happy because:
_____
_____
_____
_____
_____

_____
_____
_____
_____
_____
_____
_____

Positive Thoughts Journal Day 5

I am happy because:
_____

_____

_____

_____

_____

_____

_____

_____

_____

_____

_____

_____

Positive Thoughts Journal Day 6

I am happy because:
_____

_____

_____

_____

_____

_____

_____

_____

_____

_____

_____

_____

Positive Thoughts Journal Day 7

I am happy because:
_____
_____
_____
_____
_____

_____
_____
_____
_____
_____
_____
_____

Positive Thoughts Journal Day 8

I am happy because:
_____
_____
_____
_____
_____

_____
_____
_____
_____
_____
_____
_____

Positive Thoughts Journal Day 9

I am happy because:
_____

_____

_____

_____

_____

_____

_____

_____

_____

_____

_____

_____

Positive Thoughts Journal Day 10

I am happy because:
_____
_____
_____
_____
_____

_____
_____
_____
_____
_____
_____
_____

Positive Thoughts Journal Day 11

I am happy because:
_____
_____
_____
_____
_____

_____
_____
_____
_____
_____
_____
_____

Positive Thoughts Journal Day 12

I am happy because:

Positive Thoughts Journal Day 13

I am happy because:
_____

_____

_____

_____

_____

_____

_____

_____

_____

_____

_____

Positive Thoughts Journal Day 14

I am happy because:
_____

_____

_____

_____

_____

_____

_____

_____

_____

_____

_____

_____

Positive Thoughts Journal Day 15

I am happy because:
_____

_____

_____

_____

_____

_____

_____

_____

_____

_____

_____

SELF-ASSESSMENT SHEET (POST)

NAME: DATE:

                            LEVEL (1-5 stars)   COMMENT:

Skill	Level (1-5 stars)	Comment
Reading	☆ ☆ ☆ ☆ ☆	_____
Writing	☆ ☆ ☆ ☆ ☆	_____
Listening	☆ ☆ ☆ ☆ ☆	_____
Speaking	☆ ☆ ☆ ☆ ☆	_____
Grammar	☆ ☆ ☆ ☆ ☆	_____
Vocabulary	☆ ☆ ☆ ☆ ☆	_____
Spelling	☆ ☆ ☆ ☆ ☆	_____
Presentations	☆ ☆ ☆ ☆ ☆	_____
Overall Fluency	☆ ☆ ☆ ☆ ☆	_____

TEXTBOOK ASSESSMENT

1. Did this textbook (Optimal Levels!) help improve your English?   YES / NO

2. Comment:

3. What did you like about this textbook?

4. Which 'flavor' are you most interested in for your next textbook? (circle)

    Fun Flavor   Medical Flavor   Business Flavor

    Festival Flavor   Philosophical Flavor   Original Flavor

    Other _____   WHY? _____

NOTES

NOTES